Regal Peacocks Lace Curtain Filet Crochet Pattern

Regal Peacocks Lace Curtain Filet Crochet Pattern

Complete Instructions and Chart

designed by Olive F. Ashcroft

edited by Claudia Botterweg

EIGHTTHREEPRESS
Phoenix, Arizona, USA

for Aunt Maude

Original pattern design by Olive F. Ashcroft, first published in 1924
Pattern rewritten, expanded, edited and charted by Claudia Botterweg,
published in 2014 by Eight Three Press
ISBN-13: 978-1500108861
ISBN-10: 1500108863:
Every effort has been made to ensure that all the infor-
mation in this book is accurate. If you have questions or
comments about this pattern, please contact Claudia Botterweg at
http://claudiabotterweg.com/contact

Contents

Introduction

The peacock is a well liked motif for filet crochet, and is used in a particularly novel and attractive arrangement such as a scarf end, or, if you please, a chair-back.

The pattern is worked from the center out to one side, and then from the center to the other side.

Instructions and chart for a curtain with a straight top have been added by the editor.

Size & Yardage

The approximate size of the finished piece will change when made with different sizes of thread and hooks. Approximate yardage needed for each thread size varies also.

For best results, make a gauge swatch before you begin.

Size 5 thread (about 3.6 squares/inch)
Width: 33 ¼", Height: 22"
Amount of thread required: 1,500 yards
Suggested hook: Size 3 steel

Size 10 thread (about 4.3 squares/inch)
Width: 26", Height: 18"
Amount of thread required: 950 yards
Suggested hook: Size 7 steel

Size 20 thread (about 4.5 squares/inch)
Width: 25", Height: 17 ⅓"
Amount of thread required: 900 yards
Suggested hook: Size 10 steel

Size 30 thread (about 4.7 squares/inch)
Width: 24", Height: 16 ½"
Amount of thread required: 835 yards
Suggested hook: Size 11 steel

Size 50 thread (about 6 squares/inch)
   Width: 18 ¾", Height: 12 ⅔"
   Amount of thread required: 480 yards
   Suggested hook: Size 12 steel

Size 80 thread (about 7 squares/inch)
   Width: 16 ⅔", Height: 11"
   Amount of thread required: 375 yards
   Suggested hook: Size 14 steel

Scarf End Written Instructions

Abbreviations used in this pattern
   ( ) work instructions within parentheses as many times as directed
   * * work instructions within asterisks as many times as directed
   ch: chain stitch
   sc: single crochet
   dc: double crochet
   sk: skip the indicated amount of stitches
   sl st: slip stitch

This pattern is worked starting from the center out, then the other side is worked from Row 2 out.

   Increases are made with a foundation chain at the beginning of a row.

   Decreases are made by simply leaving squares unworked at the end of a row.

Chain 176.
   Row 1: Dc in 8th st from hook, (ch 2, sk 2, dc in next st) 41 times, 3 dc, ch 2, sk 2, dc in next st, 12 dc, (ch 2, sk 2, dc in next st) 7 times, 3 dc, ch 2, sk 2, dc in next st, turn. 57 squares.
   Row 2: Ch 5, dc in next dc, 3 dc, (ch 2, sk 2, dc in next st) 8 times, 6 dc, (ch 2, sk 2, dc in next st) 3 times, 3 dc, (ch 2, sk 2, dc in next st) 11 times, 9 dc, (ch 2, sk 2, dc in next st) 25 times, 3 dc, ch 2, sk 2, dc in next st, turn.
   Row 3: Ch 5, dc in next dc, 3 dc, (ch 2, sk 2, dc in next st) 24 times, 3 dc, (ch 2, sk 2, dc in next st) 3 times, 3 dc, (ch 2, sk 2, dc in

next st) 10 times, 3 dc, (ch 2, sk 2, dc in next st) 13 times, 3 dc, ch 2, sk 2, dc in next st, turn.

Row 4: Ch 5, dc in next dc, ch 2, sk 2, dc in next st, 3 dc, (ch 2, sk 2, dc in next st) 13 times, 3 dc, (ch 2, sk 2, dc in next st) 14 times, 3 dc, ch 2, sk 2, dc in next st, 6 dc, (ch 2, sk 2, dc in next st) 22 times, turn.

Row 5: Ch 5, dc in next dc, 3 dc, (ch 2, sk 2, dc in next st) 19 times, 3 dc, (ch 2, sk 2, dc in next st) 2 times, 3 dc, (ch 2, sk 2, dc in next st) 10 times, (ch 2, sk 2, dc in next st) 2 times, 6 dc, ch 2, sk 2, dc in next st, 6 dc, (ch 2, sk 2, dc in next st) 11 times, 3 dc, ch 2, sk 2, dc in next st, turn. 56 squares.

Row 6: Ch 5, dc in next dc, ch 2, sk 2, dc in next st, 3 dc, (ch 2, sk 2, dc in next st) 9 times, 3 dc, (ch 2, sk 2, dc in next st) 5 times, 6 dc, (ch 2, sk 2, dc in next st) 8 times, 6 dc, ch 2, sk 2, dc in next st, 3 dc, (ch 2, sk 2, dc in next st) 10 times, 3 dc, (ch 2, sk 2, dc in next st) 11 times, 3 dc, ch 2, sk 2, dc in next st, turn.

Row 7: Ch 5, dc in next dc, (ch 2, sk 2, dc in next st) 8 times, 9 dc, (ch 2, sk 2, dc in next st) 2 times, 3 dc, ch 2, sk 2, dc in next st, 3 dc, (ch 2, sk 2, dc in next st) 8 times, 3 dc, (ch 2, sk 2, dc in next st) 2 times, 3 dc, (ch 2, sk 2, dc in next st) 5 times, 6 dc, (ch 2, sk 2, dc in next st) 2 times, 6 dc, (ch 2, sk 2, dc in next st) 12 times, 6 dc, ch 2, sk 2, dc in next st, turn. 55 squares.

Row 8: Ch 5, dc in next dc, (ch 2, sk 2, dc in next st) 2 times, 3 dc, (ch 2, sk 2, dc in next st) 10 times, 3 dc, (ch 2, sk 2, dc in next st) 6 times, 3 dc, (ch 2, sk 2, dc in next st) 7 times, 3 dc, (ch 2, sk 2, dc in next st) 9 times, 3 dc, ch 2, sk 2, dc in next st, 6 dc, (ch 2, sk 2, dc in next st) 3 times, 3 dc, (ch 2, sk 2, dc in next st) 6 times, 3 dc, ch 2, sk 2, dc in next st, turn.

Row 9: Ch 5, dc in next dc, 3 dc, (ch 2, sk 2, dc in next st) 13 times, 3 dc, (ch 2, sk 2, dc in next st) 9 times, 3 dc, (ch 2, sk 2, dc in next st) 6 times, 3 dc, ch 2, sk 2, dc in next st, 9 dc, (ch 2, sk 2, dc in next st) 14 times, 3 dc, ch 2, sk 2, dc in next st, turn. 53 squares.

Row 10: Ch 5, dc in next dc, 3 dc, (ch 2, sk 2, dc in next st) 18 times, 3 dc, (ch 2, sk 2, dc in next st) 6 times, 3 dc, (ch 2, sk 2, dc in next st) 9 times, 3 dc, (ch 2, sk 2, dc in next st) 15 times, turn.

Row 11: Ch 5, dc in next dc, 3 dc, (ch 2, sk 2, dc in next st) 10 times, 9 dc, ch 2, sk 2, dc in next st, 3 dc, (ch 2, sk 2, dc in next st) 3 times, 6 dc, *(ch 2, sk 2, dc in next st) 4 times, 3 dc* twice, (ch 2, sk 2, dc in next st) 19 times, 3 dc, ch 2, sk 2, dc in next st, turn.

Row 12: Ch 11, dc in 8th st from hook, ch 2, dc in last dc of preceding row (to increase 2 spaces), ch 2, sk 2, dc in next st, 3 dc, (ch 2, sk 2, dc in next st) 15 times, 9 dc, ch 2, sk 2, dc in next st, 3 dc, (ch 2, sk 2, dc in next st) 2 times, 3 dc, ch 2, sk 2, dc in next st, 3 dc, (ch 2, sk 2, dc in next st) 3 times, 3 dc, *(ch 2, sk 2, dc in next st) 2 times, 3 dc* twice, (ch 2, sk 2, dc in next st) 4 times, 3 dc, (ch 2, sk 2, dc in next st) 9 times, 3 dc, ch 2, sk 2, dc in next st, turn. 55 squares.

Row 13: Ch 5, dc in next dc, (ch 2, sk 2, dc in next st) 14 times, 3 dc, ch 2, sk 2, dc in next st, 6 dc, (ch 2, sk 2, dc in next st) 8 times, 3 dc, (ch 2, sk 2, dc in next st) 2 times, 3 dc, (ch 2, sk 2, dc in next st) 5 times, 3 dc, (ch 2, sk 2, dc in next st) 15 times, 6 dc, ch 2, sk 2, dc in next st, turn.

Row 14: Ch 14, dc in 8th st from hook, ch 2, sk 2, dc in next st 1 time on chain, ch 2, dc in last dc of preceding row (to increase 3 spaces), ch 2, sk 2, dc in next st, 3 dc, (ch 2, sk 2, dc in next st) 22 times, 3 dc, ch 2, sk 2, dc in next st, 3 dc, (ch 2, sk 2, dc in next st) 8 times, 3 dc, (ch 2, sk 2, dc in next st) 4 times, 3 dc, (ch 2, sk 2, dc in next st) 12 times, 3 dc, ch 2, sk 2, dc in next st, turn. 58 squares.

Row 15: Ch 23, dc in 8th st from hook, (ch 2, sk 2, dc in next st) 4 more times on ch, ch 2, dc in last dc of preceding row (to increase 6 spaces), ch 2, sk 2, dc in next st, 3 dc, (ch 2, sk 2, dc in next st) 12 times, 3 dc, (ch 2, sk 2, dc in next st) 5 times, 3 dc, (ch 2, sk 2, dc in next st) 8 times, 3 dc, (ch 2, sk 2, dc in next st) 2 times, 6 dc, (ch 2, sk 2, dc in next st) 8 times, 3 dc, ch 2, sk 2, dc in next st, 3 dc, (ch 2, sk 2, dc in next st) 9 times, 9 dc, ch 2, sk 2, dc in next st, turn. 64 squares.

Row 16: Ch 14, dc in 8th st from hook, ch 2, sk 2, dc in next st 1 time on chain, ch 2, dc in last dc of preceding row (to increase 3 spaces), ch 2, sk 2, dc in next st, 3 dc, (ch 2, sk 2, dc in next st) 9 times, *3 dc, (ch 2, sk 2, dc in next st) 5 times* twice, 3 dc, (ch 2, sk 2, dc in next st) 2 times, 3 dc, ch 2, sk 2, dc in next st, 3 dc, (ch 2, sk 2, dc in next st) 4 times, 9 dc, ch 2, sk 2, dc in next st, 3 dc, (ch 2, sk 2, dc in next st) 4 times, 3 dc, (ch 2, sk 2, dc in next st) 14 times, 6 dc, ch 2, sk 2, dc in next st, 9 dc, ch 2, sk 2, dc in next st, turn. 67 squares.

Row 17: Ch 14, dc in 8th st from hook, ch 2, sk 2, dc in next st 1 time on chain, ch 2, dc in last dc of preceding row (to increase 3 spaces), ch 2, sk 2, dc in next st, 3 dc, (ch 2, sk 2, dc in next st) 25 times, 3 dc, (ch 2, sk 2, dc in next st) 3 times, 3 dc, (ch 2, sk 2, dc in next st) 2 times, 3 dc, ch 2, sk 2, dc in next st, 3 dc, (ch 2, sk 2, dc in next st) 11 times, 9 dc, (ch 2, sk 2, dc in next st) 3 times, 3 dc, ch 2, sk 2, dc in next st, 3 dc, (ch 2, sk 2, dc in next st) 6 times, 9 dc, ch 2, sk 2, dc in next st, turn. 70 squares.

Row 18: Ch 5, dc in next dc, 3 dc, (ch 2, sk 2, dc in next st) 13 times, 15 dc, ch 2, sk 2, dc in next st, 3 dc, (ch 2, sk 2, dc in next st) 8 times, 3 dc, (ch 2, sk 2, dc in next st) 35 times, 9 dc, ch 2, sk 2, dc in next st, turn.

Row 19: Ch 11, dc in 8th st from hook, ch 2, dc in last dc of preceding row (to increase 2 spaces), ch 2, sk 2, dc in next st, 3 dc, (ch 2, sk 2, dc in next st) 24 times, 15 dc, (ch 2, sk 2, dc in next st) 8 times, 3 dc, (ch 2, sk 2, dc in next st) 5 times, 3 dc, (ch 2, sk 2, dc in next st) 3 times, *6 dc, (ch 2, sk 2, dc in next st) 2 times* twice, 9 dc, ch 2, sk 2, dc in next st, 3 dc, (ch 2, sk 2, dc in next st) 6 times, 3 dc, ch 2, sk 2, dc in next st, turn. 72 squares.

Row 20: Ch 11, dc in 8th st from hook, ch 2, dc in last dc of preceding row (to increase 2 spaces), ch 2, sk 2, dc in next st, 3 dc, (ch 2, sk 2, dc in next st) 7 times, 15 dc, ch 2, sk 2, dc in next st, 6 dc, ch 2, sk 2, dc in next st, 9 dc, ch 2, sk 2, dc in next st, 3 dc, (ch 2, sk 2, dc in next st) 3 times, 3 dc, (ch 2, sk 2, dc in next st) 4 times,

3 dc, (ch 2, sk 2, dc in next st) 6 times, 30 dc, (ch 2, sk 2, dc in next st) 21 times, 6 dc, ch 2, sk 2, dc in next st, turn. 74 squares.

Row 21: Ch 8, dc in last dc of preceding row (to increase 1 space), ch 2, sk 2, dc in next st, 3 dc, (ch 2, sk 2, dc in next st) 16 times, 3 dc, (ch 2, sk 2, dc in next st) 3 times, 39 dc, (ch 2, sk 2, dc in next st) 5 times, 3 dc, (ch 2, sk 2, dc in next st) 5 times, 9 dc, (ch 2, sk 2, dc in next st) 2 times, 15 dc, ch 2, sk 2, dc in next st, 6 dc, (ch 2, sk 2, dc in next st) 2 times, 6 dc, ch 2, sk 2, dc in next st, 3 dc, (ch 2, sk 2, dc in next st) 6 times, 6 dc, ch 2, sk 2, dc in next st, turn. 75 squares.

Row 22: Ch 5, dc in next dc, 3 dc, (ch 2, sk 2, dc in next st) 9 times, 6 dc, ch 2, sk 2, dc in next st, 9 dc, *ch 2, sk 2, dc in next st, 6 dc* twice, ch 2, sk 2, dc in next st, 15 dc, ch 2, sk 2, dc in next st, 3 dc, (ch 2, sk 2, dc in next st) 2 times, 3 dc, (ch 2, sk 2, dc in next st) 5 times, 42 dc, (ch 2, sk 2, dc in next st) 2 times, 6 dc, ch 2, sk 2, dc in next st, 6 dc, (ch 2, sk 2, dc in next st) 13 times, 3 dc, ch 2, sk 2, dc in next st, turn.

Row 23: Ch 8, dc in last dc of preceding row (to increase 1 space), ch 2, sk 2, dc in next st, 3 dc, (ch 2, sk 2, dc in next st) 11 times, 6 dc, (ch 2, sk 2, dc in next st) 2 times, 3 dc, ch 2, sk 2, dc in next st, 51 dc, (ch 2, sk 2, dc in next st) 9 times, 6 dc, (ch 2, sk 2, dc in next st) 2 times, 6 dc, ch 2, sk 2, dc in next st, 3 dc, *ch 2, sk 2, dc in next st, 6 dc* twice, ch 2, sk 2, dc in next st, 12 dc, (ch 2, sk 2, dc in next st) 3 times, 3 dc, ch 2, sk 2, dc in next st, 3 dc, (ch 2, sk 2, dc in next st) 3 times, 3 dc, ch 2, sk 2, dc in next st, turn. 76 squares.

Row 24: Ch 11, dc in 8th st from hook, ch 2, dc in last dc of preceding row (to increase 2 spaces), ch 2, sk 2, dc in next st, 3 dc, (ch 2, sk 2, dc in next st) 6 times, 9 dc, ch 2, sk 2, dc in next st, 18 dc, ch 2, sk 2, dc in next st, 6 dc, ch 2, sk 2, dc in next st, 3 dc, ch 2, sk 2, dc in next st, 6 dc, ch 2, sk 2, dc in next st, 9 dc, (ch 2, sk 2, dc in next st) 3 times, 3 dc, (ch 2, sk 2, dc in next st) 4 times, 30 dc, (ch 2, sk 2, dc in next st) 3 times, 21 dc, ch 2, sk 2, dc in next st, 3 dc, (ch 2, sk 2, dc in next st) 2 times, 3 dc, (ch 2, sk 2, dc in next st) 11 times, 3 dc, ch 2, sk 2, dc in next st, turn. 78 squares.

Row 25: Ch 8, dc in last dc of preceding row (to increase 1 space), ch 2, sk 2, dc in next st, 3 dc, (ch 2, sk 2, dc in next st) 13 times, *3 dc, ch 2, sk 2, dc in next st* twice, 6 dc, (ch 2, sk 2, dc in next st) 8 times, 6 dc, (ch 2, sk 2, dc in next st) 2 times, 27 dc, (ch 2, sk 2, dc in next st) 3 times, 18 dc, ch 2, sk 2, dc in next st, 12 dc, ch 2, sk 2, dc in next st, 6 dc, ch 2, sk 2, dc in next st, 9 dc, ch 2, sk 2, dc in next st, 15 dc, ch 2, sk 2, dc in next st, 3 dc, (ch 2, sk 2, dc in next st) 4 times, 6 dc, ch 2, sk 2, dc in next st, turn. 79 squares.

Row 26: Ch 5, dc in next dc, 3 dc, (ch 2, sk 2, dc in next st) 7 times, 3 dc, (ch 2, sk 2, dc in next st) 2 times, 9 dc, *ch 2, sk 2, dc in next st, 6 dc* twice, ch 2, sk 2, dc in next st, 12 dc, ch 2, sk 2, dc in next st, 9 dc, ch 2, sk 2, dc in next st, 6 dc, (ch 2, sk 2, dc in next st) 2 times, 3 dc, (ch 2, sk 2, dc in next st) 3 times, 15 dc, ch 2, sk 2, dc in next st, 9 dc, (ch 2, sk 2, dc in next st) 11 times, *3 dc, ch 2, sk 2, dc in next st* twice, 6 dc, (ch 2, sk 2, dc in next st) 12 times, 3 dc, ch 2, sk 2, dc in next st, turn.

Row 27: Ch 5, dc in next dc, 3 dc, (ch 2, sk 2, dc in next st) 11 times, 3 dc, (ch 2, sk 2, dc in next st) 3 times, 3 dc, ch 2, sk 2, dc in next st, 3 dc, (ch 2, sk 2, dc in next st) 11 times, 12 dc, ch 2, sk 2, dc in next st, 6 dc, (ch 2, sk 2, dc in next st) 4 times, 3 dc, (ch 2, sk 2, dc in next st) 3 times, 3 dc, ch 2, sk 2, dc in next st, 9 dc, ch 2, sk 2, dc in next st, 12 dc, *ch 2, sk 2, dc in next st, 6 dc* twice, ch 2, sk 2, dc in next st, 15 dc, *ch 2, sk 2, dc in next st, 3 dc* twice, (ch 2, sk 2, dc in next st) 5 times, 3 dc, ch 2, sk 2, dc in next st, turn.

Row 28: Ch 5, dc in next dc, 3 dc, (ch 2, sk 2, dc in next st) 7 times, 9 dc, *ch 2, sk 2, dc in next st, 12 dc, ch 2, sk 2, dc in next st, 15 dc* twice, (ch 2, sk 2, dc in next st) 3 times, 18 dc, ch 2, sk 2, dc in next st, 12 dc, (ch 2, sk 2, dc in next st) 10 times, 3 dc, (ch 2, sk 2, dc in next st) 2 times, 3 dc, (ch 2, sk 2, dc in next st) 17 times, turn.

Row 29: Ch 5, dc in next dc, 3 dc, (ch 2, sk 2, dc in next st) 14 times, 3 dc, (ch 2, sk 2, dc in next st) 13 times, 15 dc, ch 2, sk 2, dc in next st, 9 dc, (ch 2, sk 2, dc in next st) 3 times, 3 dc, *(ch 2, sk 2, dc in next st) 2 times, 9 dc* twice, (ch 2, sk 2, dc in next st) 2 times,

15 dc, ch 2, sk 2, dc in next st, 12 dc, ch 2, sk 2, dc in next st, 9 dc, ch 2, sk 2, dc in next st, 3 dc, (ch 2, sk 2, dc in next st) 6 times, 3 dc, ch 2, sk 2, dc in next st, turn.

Row 30: Ch 5, dc in next dc, 3 dc, (ch 2, sk 2, dc in next st) 8 times, 12 dc, (ch 2, sk 2, dc in next st) 2 times, 9 dc, ch 2, sk 2, dc in next st, 18 dc, ch 2, sk 2, dc in next st, 12 dc, (ch 2, sk 2, dc in next st) 2 times, 6 dc, (ch 2, sk 2, dc in next st) 6 times, 3 dc, ch 2, sk 2, dc in next st, 18 dc, (ch 2, sk 2, dc in next st) 28 times, 3 dc, ch 2, sk 2, dc in next st, turn.

Row 31: Ch 5, dc in next dc, (ch 2, sk 2, dc in next st) 29 times, 18 dc, ch 2, sk 2, dc in next st, 6 dc, (ch 2, sk 2, dc in next st) 4 times, 6 dc, *ch 2, sk 2, dc in next st, 15 dc* twice, (ch 2, sk 2, dc in next st) 2 times, 9 dc, ch 2, sk 2, dc in next st, 15 dc, ch 2, sk 2, dc in next st, 3 dc, (ch 2, sk 2, dc in next st) 7 times, 3 dc, ch 2, sk 2, dc in next st, turn.

Row 32: Ch 5, dc in next dc, 3 dc, (ch 2, sk 2, dc in next st) 11 times, 27 dc, (ch 2, sk 2, dc in next st) 2 times, 12 dc, ch 2, sk 2, dc in next st, 15 dc, ch 2, sk 2, dc in next st, 21 dc, ch 2, sk 2, dc in next st, 18 dc, (ch 2, sk 2, dc in next st) 28 times, 3 dc, ch 2, sk 2, dc in next st, turn.

Row 33: Ch 5, dc in next dc, 3 dc, (ch 2, sk 2, dc in next st) 15 times, 3 dc, (ch 2, sk 2, dc in next st) 13 times, 18 dc, ch 2, sk 2, dc in next st, 48 dc, ch 2, sk 2, dc in next st, 27 dc, (ch 2, sk 2, dc in next st) 13 times, 3 dc, ch 2, sk 2, dc in next st, turn.

Row 34: Ch 5, dc in next dc, 3 dc, (ch 2, sk 2, dc in next st) 8 times, 3 dc, ch 2, sk 2, dc in next st, 18 dc, (ch 2, sk 2, dc in next st) 3 times, 57 dc, ch 2, sk 2, dc in next st, 21 dc, (ch 2, sk 2, dc in next st) 10 times, 3 dc, (ch 2, sk 2, dc in next st) 3 times, 3 dc, (ch 2, sk 2, dc in next st) 16 times, turn.

Row 35: Ch 5, dc in next dc, 3 dc, (ch 2, sk 2, dc in next st) 9 times, *3 dc, (ch 2, sk 2, dc in next st) 4 times* twice, 6 dc, (ch 2, sk 2, dc in next st) 3 times, 3 dc, (ch 2, sk 2, dc in next st) 5 times, *9 dc, ch 2, sk 2, dc in next st* twice, 30 dc, (ch 2, sk 2, dc in next st)

3 times, 12 dc, ch 2, sk 2, dc in next st, 9 dc, (ch 2, sk 2, dc in next st) 3 times, 12 dc, (ch 2, sk 2, dc in next st) 9 times, 3 dc, ch 2, sk 2, dc in next st, turn.

Row 36: Ch 5, dc in next dc, 3 dc, (ch 2, sk 2, dc in next st) 7 times, 3 dc, ch 2, sk 2, dc in next st, 6 dc, ch 2, sk 2, dc in next st, 33 dc, ch 2, sk 2, dc in next st, 9 dc, (ch 2, sk 2, dc in next st) 4 times, 21 dc, (ch 2, sk 2, dc in next st) 3 times, 9 dc, (ch 2, sk 2, dc in next st) 7 times, 3 dc, ch 2, sk 2, dc in next st, 3 dc, (ch 2, sk 2, dc in next st) 3 times, 9 dc, (ch 2, sk 2, dc in next st) 3 times, 6 dc, (ch 2, sk 2, dc in next st) 10 times, 3 dc, ch 2, sk 2, dc in next st, turn.

Row 37: Ch 5, dc in next dc, (ch 2, sk 2, dc in next st) 5 times, 3 dc, (ch 2, sk 2, dc in next st) 7 times, 9 dc, (ch 2, sk 2, dc in next st) 3 times, 6 dc, (ch 2, sk 2, dc in next st) 3 times, 3 dc, (ch 2, sk 2, dc in next st) 8 times, 24 dc, (ch 2, sk 2, dc in next st) 4 times, 30 dc, (ch 2, sk 2, dc in next st) 4 times, 12 dc, (ch 2, sk 2, dc in next st) 2 times, 6 dc, (ch 2, sk 2, dc in next st) 8 times, 6 dc, ch 2, sk 2, dc in next st, turn.

Row 38: Ch 5, dc in next dc, (ch 2, sk 2, dc in next st) 2 times, 3 dc, (ch 2, sk 2, dc in next st) 6 times, 3 dc, ch 2, sk 2, dc in next st, 15 dc, (ch 2, sk 2, dc in next st) 2 times, 12 dc, ch 2, sk 2, dc in next st, 60 dc, (ch 2, sk 2, dc in next st) 8 times, 3 dc, (ch 2, sk 2, dc in next st) 2 times, 6 dc, (ch 2, sk 2, dc in next st) 2 times, 9 dc, (ch 2, sk 2, dc in next st) 3 times, 3 dc, (ch 2, sk 2, dc in next st) 4 times, 6 dc, (ch 2, sk 2, dc in next st) 5 times, 3 dc, ch 2, sk 2, dc in next st, turn.

Row 39: Ch 5, dc in next dc, 3 dc, (ch 2, sk 2, dc in next st) 7 times, 12 dc, (ch 2, sk 2, dc in next st) 2 times, 6 dc, (ch 2, sk 2, dc in next st) 4 times, 3 dc, (ch 2, sk 2, dc in next st) 2 times, 6 dc, (ch 2, sk 2, dc in next st) 10 times, 63 dc, ch 2, sk 2, dc in next st, 12 dc, ch 2, sk 2, dc in next st, 9 dc, (ch 2, sk 2, dc in next st) 9 times, 3 dc, ch 2, sk 2, dc in next st, turn. 77 squares.

Row 40: Ch 5, dc in next dc, 3 dc, (ch 2, sk 2, dc in next st) 8 times, 3 dc, (ch 2, sk 2, dc in next st) 3 times, 9 dc, (ch 2, sk 2, dc in next st) 2 times, 15 dc, (ch 2, sk 2, dc in next st) 6 times, 24 dc, (ch

2, sk 2, dc in next st) 3 times, 3 dc, (ch 2, sk 2, dc in next st) 7 times, 6 dc, (ch 2, sk 2, dc in next st) 5 times, 6 dc, (ch 2, sk 2, dc in next st) 4 times, 3 dc, (ch 2, sk 2, dc in next st) 14 times, turn.

Row 41: Ch 5, dc in next dc, 3 dc, (ch 2, sk 2, dc in next st) 9 times, 6 dc, ch 2, sk 2, dc in next st, 3 dc, (ch 2, sk 2, dc in next st) 3 times, 3 dc, (ch 2, sk 2, dc in next st) 5 times, 6 dc, (ch 2, sk 2, dc in next st) 2 times, 6 dc, (ch 2, sk 2, dc in next st) 4 times, 3 dc, (ch 2, sk 2, dc in next st) 17 times, 3 dc, (ch 2, sk 2, dc in next st) 2 times, 18 dc, ch 2, sk 2, dc in next st, 6 dc, (ch 2, sk 2, dc in next st) 10 times, 6 dc, ch 2, sk 2, dc in next st, turn.

Row 42: Ch 5, dc in next dc, (ch 2, sk 2, dc in next st) 2 times, 3 dc, (ch 2, sk 2, dc in next st) 7 times, 3 dc, ch 2, sk 2, dc in next st, 6 dc, (ch 2, sk 2, dc in next st) 2 times, 12 dc, ch 2, sk 2, dc in next st, 3 dc, (ch 2, sk 2, dc in next st) 19 times, 3 dc, (ch 2, sk 2, dc in next st) 3 times, 3 dc, (ch 2, sk 2, dc in next st) 6 times, 6 dc, (ch 2, sk 2, dc in next st) 7 times, 3 dc, (ch 2, sk 2, dc in next st) 3 times, 6 dc, (ch 2, sk 2, dc in next st) 7 times, 3 dc, ch 2, sk 2, dc in next st, turn.

Row 43: Ch 5, dc in next dc, (ch 2, sk 2, dc in next st) 7 times, 3 dc, (ch 2, sk 2, dc in next st) 6 times, 3 dc, (ch 2, sk 2, dc in next st) 5 times, 3 dc, (ch 2, sk 2, dc in next st) 9 times, *3 dc, (ch 2, sk 2, dc in next st) 2 times* twice, 3 dc, (ch 2, sk 2, dc in next st) 4 times, 3 dc, (ch 2, sk 2, dc in next st) 14 times, 21 dc, (ch 2, sk 2, dc in next st) 9 times, 3 dc, ch 2, sk 2, dc in next st, turn. 75 squares.

Row 44: Ch 5, dc in next dc, 3 dc, (ch 2, sk 2, dc in next st) 8 times, 3 dc, (ch 2, sk 2, dc in next st) 2 times, 12 dc, ch 2, sk 2, dc in next st, 3 dc, (ch 2, sk 2, dc in next st) 14 times, 6 dc, (ch 2, sk 2, dc in next st) 2 times, 3 dc, (ch 2, sk 2, dc in next st) 3 times, 3 dc, ch 2, sk 2, dc in next st, 3 dc, (ch 2, sk 2, dc in next st) 29 times, 3 dc, ch 2, sk 2, dc in next st, turn.

Row 45: Ch 5, dc in next dc, 3 dc, (ch 2, sk 2, dc in next st) 23 times, 6 dc, (ch 2, sk 2, dc in next st) 4 times, 3 dc, ch 2, sk 2, dc in next st, 3 dc, (ch 2, sk 2, dc in next st) 2 times, 3 dc, ch 2, sk 2, dc in next st, 6 dc, (ch 2, sk 2, dc in next st) 22 times, 3 dc, (ch 2, sk 2, dc in next st) 8 times, 9 dc, ch 2, sk 2, dc in next st, turn.

Row 46: Ch 5, dc in next dc, (ch 2, sk 2, dc in next st) 3 times, 3 dc, (ch 2, sk 2, dc in next st) 9 times, 3 dc, ch 2, sk 2, dc in next st, 3 dc, (ch 2, sk 2, dc in next st) 17 times, 3 dc, (ch 2, sk 2, dc in next st) 4 times, *3 dc, ch 2, sk 2, dc in next st* twice, *3 dc, (ch 2, sk 2, dc in next st) 2 times* twice, 6 dc, (ch 2, sk 2, dc in next st) 24 times, turn.

Row 47: Ch 5, dc in next dc, 3 dc, (ch 2, sk 2, dc in next st) 27 times, 3 dc, (ch 2, sk 2, dc in next st) 2 times, 3 dc, ch 2, sk 2, dc in next st, 3 dc, (ch 2, sk 2, dc in next st) 33 times, 9 dc, ch 2, sk 2, dc in next st, turn. 72 squares.

Row 48: Ch 5, dc in next dc, (ch 2, sk 2, dc in next st) 3 times, 3 dc, (ch 2, sk 2, dc in next st) 35 times, 3 dc, ch 2, sk 2, dc in next st, 3 dc, (ch 2, sk 2, dc in next st) 27 times, 3 dc, ch 2, sk 2, dc in next st, turn.

Row 49: Ch 5, dc in next dc, (ch 2, sk 2, dc in next st) 30 times, 3 dc, (ch 2, sk 2, dc in next st) 34 times, 6 dc, ch 2, sk 2, dc in next st, turn. 69 squares.

Row 50: Ch 5, dc in next dc, (ch 2, sk 2, dc in next st) 2 times, 3 dc, (ch 2, sk 2, dc in next st) 63 times, 3 dc, ch 2, sk 2, dc in next st, turn.

Row 51: Ch 5, dc in next dc, *6 dc, ch 2, sk 2, dc in next st* 22 times, turn. 67 squares.

Row 52: Ch 5, dc in next dc, (ch 2, sk 2, dc in next st) 66 times.

This completes one half of the scarf-end. Fasten in at end of 1st row and repeat from Row 2 for the other half. Do not break the thread after finishing the last row of second half, but turn and work the edge.

Edge

The edge is finished with single crochet and picots on the outside and bottom edges of the lace.

Work 3 sc in space, picot of 5 chain, * 3 sc in each of 3 spaces, picot over dc; repeat from * down the side, * in corner space work 3 sc, picot, 3 sc, fill each space to next corner with 3 sc, repeat from last * 5 times, then work across bottom of scallop as at first, and continue, putting a picot in each corner space, and a picot over 4th space at bottom of small middle scallop.

Scarf End Chart

Chain 176.

This pattern is worked starting from the center out, then the other side is worked from Row 2 out.

Odd rows are worked left to right. Even rows are worked right to left.

Begin rows that start with a space with ch 5.

Increases are made with a foundation chain at the beginning of a row. See written instructions for details.

Decreases are made by simply leaving squares unworked at the end of a row.

Regal Peacocks Lace Curtain

Curtain Written Instructions

This pattern is worked starting from the center out, then the other side is worked from Row 2 out.

Increases are made with a foundation chain at the beginning of a row.

Decreases are made by simply leaving squares unworked.

Chain 218.

Row 1: Dc in 8th st from hook, (ch 2, sk 2, dc in next st) 55 times, 3 dc, ch 2, sk 2, dc in next st, 12 dc, (ch 2, sk 2, dc in next st) 7 times, 3 dc, ch 2, sk 2, dc in next st, turn. 71 squares.

Row 2: Ch 5, dc in next dc, 3 dc, (ch 2, sk 2, dc in next st) 8 times, 6 dc, (ch 2, sk 2, dc in next st) 3 times, 3 dc, (ch 2, sk 2, dc in next st) 11 times, 9 dc, (ch 2, sk 2, dc in next st) 39 times, 3 dc, ch 2, sk 2, dc in next st, turn.

Row 3: Ch 5, dc in next dc, 3 dc, (ch 2, sk 2, dc in next st) 38 times, 3 dc, (ch 2, sk 2, dc in next st) 3 times, 3 dc, (ch 2, sk 2, dc in next st) 10 times, 3 dc, (ch 2, sk 2, dc in next st) 13 times, 3 dc, ch 2, sk 2, dc in next st, turn.

Row 4: Ch 5, dc in next dc, ch 2, sk 2, dc in next st, 3 dc, (ch 2, sk 2, dc in next st) 13 times, 3 dc, (ch 2, sk 2, dc in next st) 14 times, 3 dc, ch 2, sk 2, dc in next st, 6 dc, (ch 2, sk 2, dc in next st) 36 times, turn.

Row 5: Ch 5, dc in next dc, 3 dc, (ch 2, sk 2, dc in next st) 33 times, 3 dc, (ch 2, sk 2, dc in next st) 2 times, 3 dc, (ch 2, sk 2, dc in next st) 10 times, 3 dc, (ch 2, sk 2, dc in next st) 2 times, 6 dc, ch 2, sk 2, dc in next st, 6 dc, (ch 2, sk 2, dc in next st) 11 times, 3 dc, ch 2, sk 2, dc in next st, turn. 70 squares.

Row 6: Ch 5, dc in next dc, ch 2, sk 2, dc in next st, 3 dc, (ch 2, sk 2, dc in next st) 9 times, 3 dc, (ch 2, sk 2, dc in next st) 5 times, 6 dc, (ch 2, sk 2, dc in next st) 8 times, 6 dc, ch 2, sk 2, dc in next st, 3 dc, (ch 2, sk 2, dc in next st) 10 times, 3 dc, (ch 2, sk 2, dc in next st) 25 times, 3 dc, ch 2, sk 2, dc in next st, turn.

Row 7: Ch 5, dc in next dc, (ch 2, sk 2, dc in next st) 22 times, 9 dc, (ch 2, sk 2, dc in next st) 2 times, 3 dc, ch 2, sk 2, dc in next st, 3 dc, (ch 2, sk 2, dc in next st) 8 times, 3 dc, (ch 2, sk 2, dc in next st) 2 times, 3 dc, (ch 2, sk 2, dc in next st) 5 times, 6 dc, (ch 2, sk 2, dc in next st) 2 times, 6 dc, (ch 2, sk 2, dc in next st) 12 times, 6 dc, ch 2, sk 2, dc in next st, turn. 69 squares.

Row 8: Ch 5, dc in next dc, (ch 2, sk 2, dc in next st) 2 times, 3 dc, (ch 2, sk 2, dc in next st) 10 times, 3 dc, (ch 2, sk 2, dc in next st) 6 times, 3 dc, (ch 2, sk 2, dc in next st) 7 times, 3 dc, (ch 2, sk 2, dc in next st) 9 times, 3 dc, ch 2, sk 2, dc in next st, 6 dc, (ch 2, sk 2, dc in next st) 3 times, 3 dc, (ch 2, sk 2, dc in next st) 20 times, 3 dc, ch 2, sk 2, dc in next st, turn.

Row 9: Ch 5, dc in next dc, 3 dc, (ch 2, sk 2, dc in next st) 27 times, 3 dc, (ch 2, sk 2, dc in next st) 9 times, 3 dc, (ch 2, sk 2, dc in next st) 6 times, 3 dc, ch 2, sk 2, dc in next st, 9 dc, (ch 2, sk 2, dc in next st) 14 times, 3 dc, ch 2, sk 2, dc in next st, turn. 67 squares.

Row 10: Ch 5, dc in next dc, 3 dc, (ch 2, sk 2, dc in next st) 18 times, 3 dc, (ch 2, sk 2, dc in next st) 6 times, 3 dc, (ch 2, sk 2, dc in next st) 9 times, 3 dc, (ch 2, sk 2, dc in next st) 29 times, turn.

Row 11: Ch 5, dc in next dc, 3 dc, (ch 2, sk 2, dc in next st) 24 times, 9 dc, ch 2, sk 2, dc in next st, 3 dc, (ch 2, sk 2, dc in next st) 3 times, 6 dc, *(ch 2, sk 2, dc in next st) 4 times, 3 dc* twice, (ch 2, sk 2, dc in next st) 19 times, 3 dc, ch 2, sk 2, dc in next st, turn.

Row 12: Ch 11, dc in 8th st from hook, ch 2, dc in last dc of preceding row (to increase 2 spaces), ch 2, sk 2, dc in next st, 3 dc, (ch 2, sk 2, dc in next st) 15 times, 9 dc, ch 2, sk 2, dc in next st, 3 dc, (ch 2, sk 2, dc in next st) 2 times, 3 dc, ch 2, sk 2, dc in next st, 3 dc, (ch 2, sk 2, dc in next st) 3 times, 3 dc, *(ch 2, sk 2, dc in next st) 2 times, 3 dc* twice, (ch 2, sk 2, dc in next st) 4 times, 3 dc, (ch 2, sk 2, dc in next st) 23 times, 3 dc, ch 2, sk 2, dc in next st, turn. 69 squares.

Row 13: Ch 5, dc in next dc, (ch 2, sk 2, dc in next st) 28 times, 3 dc, ch 2, sk 2, dc in next st, 6 dc, (ch 2, sk 2, dc in next st) 8 times, 3 dc, (ch 2, sk 2, dc in next st) 2 times, 3 dc, (ch 2, sk 2, dc in next st) 5 times, 3 dc, (ch 2, sk 2, dc in next st) 15 times, 6 dc, ch 2, sk 2, dc in next st, turn.

Row 14: Ch 14, dc in 8th st from hook, ch 2, sk 2, dc in next st 1 more time on chain, ch 2, dc in last dc of preceding row (to increase 3 spaces), ch 2, sk 2, dc in next st, 3 dc, (ch 2, sk 2, dc in next st) 22 times, 3 dc, ch 2, sk 2, dc in next st, 3 dc, (ch 2, sk 2, dc in next st) 8 times, 3 dc, (ch 2, sk 2, dc in next st) 4 times, 3 dc, (ch 2, sk 2, dc in next st) 26 times, 3 dc, ch 2, sk 2, dc in next st, turn. 72 squares.

Row 15: Ch 5, dc in next dc, 3 dc, (ch 2, sk 2, dc in next st) 26 times, 3 dc, (ch 2, sk 2, dc in next st) 5 times, 3 dc, (ch 2, sk 2, dc in next st) 8 times, 3 dc, (ch 2, sk 2, dc in next st) 2 times, 6 dc, (ch 2, sk 2, dc in next st) 8 times, 3 dc, ch 2, sk 2, dc in next st, 3 dc, (ch 2, sk 2, dc in next st) 9 times, 9 dc, ch 2, sk 2, dc in next st, turn.

Row 16: Ch 14, dc in 8th st from hook, ch 2, sk 2, dc in next st 1 more time on chain, ch 2, dc in last dc of preceding row (to increase 3 spaces), ch 2, sk 2, dc in next st, 3 dc, (ch 2, sk 2, dc in next st) 9 times, *3 dc, (ch 2, sk 2, dc in next st) 5 times* twice, 3 dc, (ch 2, sk 2, dc in next st) 2 times, 3 dc, ch 2, sk 2, dc in next st, 3 dc, (ch 2, sk 2, dc in next st) 4 times, 9 dc, ch 2, sk 2, dc in next st, 3 dc, (ch 2, sk 2, dc in next st) 4 times, 3 dc, (ch 2, sk 2, dc in next st) 29 times, turn. 75 squares.

Row 17: Ch 5, dc in next dc, 3 dc, (ch 2, sk 2, dc in next st) 33 times, 3 dc, (ch 2, sk 2, dc in next st) 3 times, 3 dc, (ch 2, sk 2, dc in next st) 2 times, 3 dc, ch 2, sk 2, dc in next st, 3 dc, (ch 2, sk 2, dc in next st) 11 times, 9 dc, (ch 2, sk 2, dc in next st) 3 times, 3 dc, ch 2, sk 2, dc in next st, 3 dc, (ch 2, sk 2, dc in next st) 6 times, 9 dc, ch 2, sk 2, dc in next st, turn.

Row 18: Ch 5, dc in next dc, 3 dc, (ch 2, sk 2, dc in next st) 13 times, 15 dc, ch 2, sk 2, dc in next st, 3 dc, (ch 2, sk 2, dc in next st) 8 times, 3 dc, (ch 2, sk 2, dc in next st) 42 times, 3 dc, ch 2, sk 2, dc in next st, turn.

Row 19: Ch 5, dc in next dc, (ch 2, sk 2, dc in next st) 30 times, 15 dc, (ch 2, sk 2, dc in next st) 8 times, 3 dc, (ch 2, sk 2, dc in next st) 5 times, 3 dc, (ch 2, sk 2, dc in next st) 3 times, *6 dc, (ch 2, sk 2, dc in next st) 2 times* twice, 9 dc, ch 2, sk 2, dc in next st, 3 dc, (ch 2, sk 2, dc in next st) 6 times, 3 dc, ch 2, sk 2, dc in next st, turn.

Row 20: Ch 11, dc in 8th st from hook, ch 2, dc in last dc of preceding row (to increase 2 spaces), ch 2, sk 2, dc in next st, 3 dc, (ch 2, sk 2, dc in next st) 7 times, 15 dc, ch 2, sk 2, dc in next st, 6 dc, ch 2, sk 2, dc in next st, 9 dc, ch 2, sk 2, dc in next st, 3 dc, (ch 2, sk 2, dc in next st) 3 times, 3 dc, (ch 2, sk 2, dc in next st) 4 times, 3 dc, (ch 2, sk 2, dc in next st) 6 times, 30 dc, (ch 2, sk 2, dc in next st) 25 times, 3 dc, ch 2, sk 2, dc in next st, turn. 77 squares.

Row 21: Ch 5, dc in next dc, 3 dc, (ch 2, sk 2, dc in next st) 19 times, 3 dc, (ch 2, sk 2, dc in next st) 3 times, 39 dc, (ch 2, sk 2, dc in next st) 5 times, 3 dc, (ch 2, sk 2, dc in next st) 5 times, 9 dc, (ch 2, sk 2, dc in next st) 2 times, 15 dc, ch 2, sk 2, dc in next st, 6 dc, (ch 2, sk 2, dc in next st) 2 times, 6 dc, ch 2, sk 2, dc in next st, 3 dc, (ch 2, sk 2, dc in next st) 6 times, 6 dc, ch 2, sk 2, dc in next st, turn.

Row 22: Ch 5, dc in next dc, 3 dc, (ch 2, sk 2, dc in next st) 9 times, 6 dc, ch 2, sk 2, dc in next st, 9 dc, *ch 2, sk 2, dc in next st, 6 dc* twice, ch 2, sk 2, dc in next st, 15 dc, ch 2, sk 2, dc in next st, 3 dc, (ch 2, sk 2, dc in next st) 2 times, 3 dc, (ch 2, sk 2, dc in next st) 5 times, 42 dc, (ch 2, sk 2, dc in next st) 2 times, 6 dc, ch 2, sk 2, dc in next st, 6 dc, (ch 2, sk 2, dc in next st) 17 times, turn.

Row 23: Ch 5, dc in next dc, 3 dc, (ch 2, sk 2, dc in next st) 13 times, 6 dc, (ch 2, sk 2, dc in next st) 2 times, 3 dc, ch 2, sk 2, dc in next st, 51 dc, (ch 2, sk 2, dc in next st) 9 times, 6 dc, (ch 2, sk 2, dc in next st) 2 times, 6 dc, ch 2, sk 2, dc in next st, 3 dc, *ch 2, sk 2, dc in next st, 6 dc* twice, ch 2, sk 2, dc in next st, 12 dc, (ch 2, sk 2, dc in next st) 3 times, 3 dc, ch 2, sk 2, dc in next st, 3 dc, (ch 2, sk 2, dc in next st) 3 times, 3 dc, ch 2, sk 2, dc in next st, turn.

Row 24: Ch 11, dc in 8th st from hook, ch 2, dc in last dc of preceding row (to increase 2 spaces), ch 2, sk 2, dc in next st, 3 dc, (ch 2, sk 2, dc in next st) 6 times, 9 dc, ch 2, sk 2, dc in next st, 18 dc, ch 2, sk 2, dc in next st, 6 dc, ch 2, sk 2, dc in next st, 3 dc, ch 2, sk 2, dc in next st, 6 dc, ch 2, sk 2, dc in next st, 9 dc, (ch 2, sk 2, dc in next st) 3 times, 3 dc, (ch 2, sk 2, dc in next st) 4 times, 30 dc, (ch 2, sk 2, dc in next st) 3 times, 21 dc, ch 2, sk 2, dc in next st, 3 dc, (ch 2, sk 2, dc in next st) 2 times, 3 dc, (ch 2, sk 2, dc in next st) 12 times, 3 dc, ch 2, sk 2, dc in next st, turn. 79 squares.

Row 25: Ch 5, dc in next dc, (ch 2, sk 2, dc in next st) 15 times, *3 dc, ch 2, sk 2, dc in next st* twice, 6 dc, (ch 2, sk 2, dc in next st) 8 times, 6 dc, (ch 2, sk 2, dc in next st) 2 times, 27 dc, (ch 2, sk 2, dc in next st) 3 times, 18 dc, ch 2, sk 2, dc in next st, 12 dc, ch 2, sk 2, dc in next st, 6 dc, ch 2, sk 2, dc in next st, 9 dc, ch 2, sk 2, dc in next st, 15 dc, ch 2, sk 2, dc in next st, 3 dc, (ch 2, sk 2, dc in next st) 4 times, 6 dc, ch 2, sk 2, dc in next st, turn.

Continue from Row 26 of Scarf End instructions, then come back to Row 2 for the other half of the curtain. When you're finished, work the Edging at the end of the scarf end instructions.

Curtain Chart

Chain 218.

This pattern is worked starting from the center out, then the other side is worked from Row 2 out.

Odd rows are worked left to right. Even rows are worked right to left.

Begin rows that start with a space with ch 5.

Increases are made with a foundation chain at the beginning of a row. See written instructions for details.

Decreases are made by simply leaving squares unworked at the end of a row.

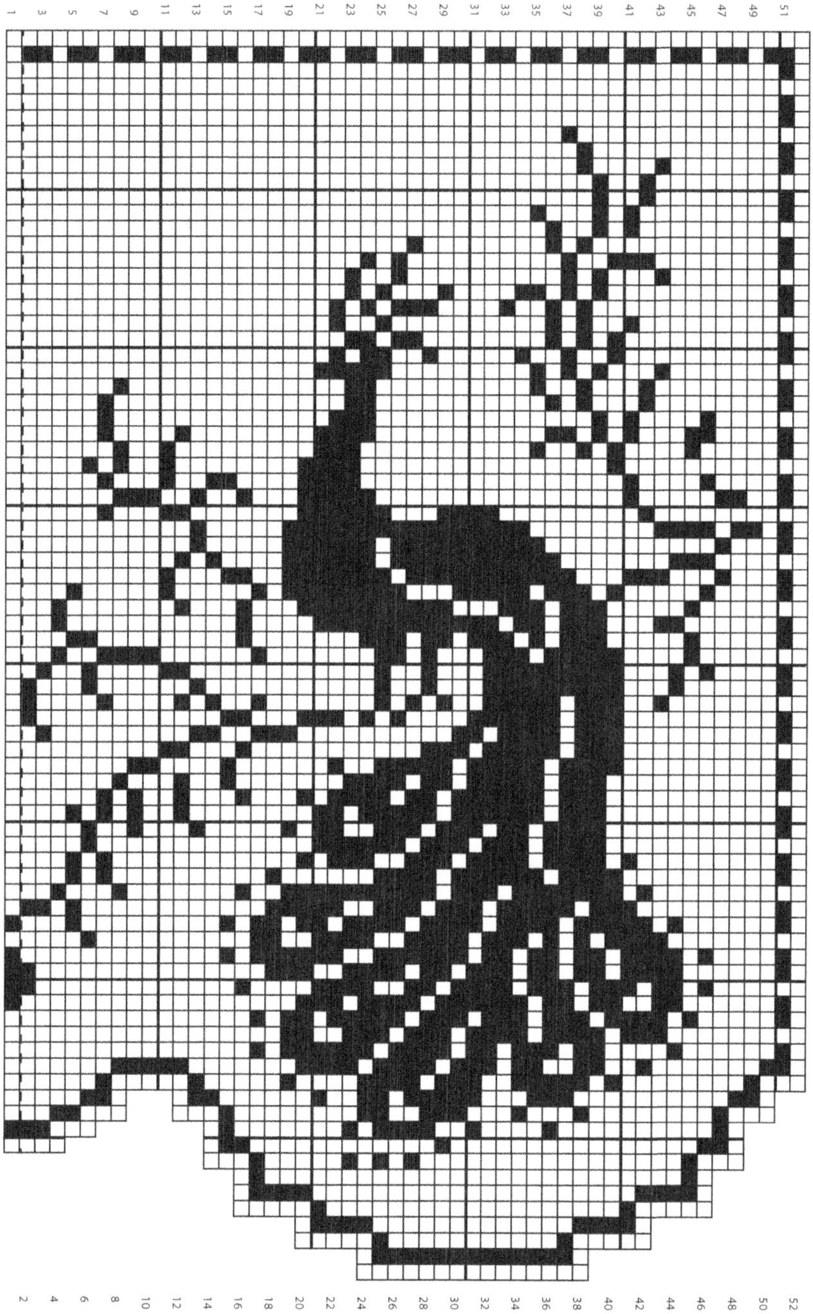

Hints & Tips

Wash your hands before you pick up your project to work on. Keeping your hands clean while you work will help to avoid stains on your piece of lace.

When you're finished, weave in ends of thread by pulling the thread through several stitches with your hook.

To block your lace, dampen it and use a warm iron to block it in to shape. I like to use a little bit of spray starch to finish it off.

Filet crochet patterns are made up of two elements. The first is the space, which is made up of a double crochet, chain two, skip two stitches, and double crochet in the next stitch. The second is the block, which is made of a double crochet, double crochet in the next two stitches, and double crochet in the next stitch.

When you make a block over a space from the previous row, just double crochet into the space. Don't worry about crocheting into each chain.

You can follow a chart instead of a written pattern (a chart is included with this pattern). When you use the chart, you just need to remember that the beginning of each row starts with either chain three (for a block) or chain five (for a space). You can also use the chart to check your progress if you're using the written instructions.

Filet crochet blocks and spaces are not quite square, so your finished project won't look as squared off as the chart.

Visit http://claudiabotterweg.com/crochet for tips, hints and more about lace crochet.

I hope you enjoyed making this beautiful piece of lace. Tell your friends where you got the pattern.

About the Editor

Claudia Botterweg learned how to crochet in third grade, and by the time she left home for college she had completed 8 rows on a ripple afghan. At Ohio State, she found herself living across the street from a vintage clothing store, and spent most of her budget on vintage clothes. She began repairing clothes in exchange for store credit. One of her tasks was to make camisoles with vintage crocheted lace yokes.

After college, Claudia inherited a tin full of several used balls of tatting thread, a tatting shuttle, and a size 14 steel crochet hook from her grandmother. She made some lace edgings from an old crochet pattern book, became fascinated with lace, and graduated to making doilies. In the 1980s, she made hundreds of lace collars and sold them at craft fairs. She also designed her own camisole yokes and made camisoles to sell.

Recently, Claudia acquired a stack of vintage patterns. She has been busily translating the patterns from vintage instructions, making them easy for beginning and intermediate crocheters to read. She is writing instructions when only charts were provided, and making charts when only written instructions were provided.

Claudia hopes that a new generation of crocheters will learn how to make beautiful lace to decorate themselves, their friends and families, and their homes.

http://ClaudiaBotterweg.com

More Patterns from Claudia Botterweg

Grape & Leaf Altar Lace
Ivy Lace Scarf End
Beverly Lace & Insertion
Dogwood Blossom Lace Curtain
Two Peacocks Lace Curtain
Quilt Block Lace Edging & Insertion
Two Dragons Lace Curtain
Lyre Lace Scarf End
Butterfly Lace Camisole Yoke
Daffodil Lace Curtain
Rose Lace & Insertion
Daffodil Altar Lace
Garden Trellis Lace Centerpiece
Elegant Dragons Lace Curtain

Printed in Great Britain
by Amazon

65101004R00020